Super Social Studies

By
Elizabeth Van Tine
Shirley Lee
Camille Cooper
Barbara White

SCHOLASTIC
PROFESSIONAL BOOKS

NEW YORK • TORONTO • LONDON • AUCKLAND • SYDNEY
MEXICO CITY • NEW DELHI • HONG KONG

Acknowledgments

We would like to thank the following teachers who so generously shared their ideas with us:
Gail Crabtree, Kathy Cameruci, and Judith McClure, Dayton Public Schools;
Liz Goheen, Vandalia City Schools; Janna Soelter, Huber Heights City Schools;
Judy Aiken, Centerville City Schools; Deb Barry, Lisa Gaylor,
Linda Reeves, and Judy Tipton, Northmont City Schools.

Cover design by Jaime Lucero
Cover photograph by Donnelly Marks
Interior design by Solutions by Design, Inc.
Interior illustration Teresa Anderko

ISBN 0-439-05008-1

Table of Contents

Research and Reporting Activities

Introduction

Shirley Lee, Barbara White, Camille Cooper, and I began to develop the ideas included in this book when the state of Ohio instituted proficiency testing in grades 4 and 6. The tests include multiple-choice, short-answer, and extended-response questions. They also include graphs, charts, timelines, graphic organizers, maps, and pictures for students to interpret. We soon realized we couldn't find any grade-appropriate materials to help our students prepare for these tests. We began developing a variety of teaching tools to support both fourth-grade and sixth-grade teachers. Our goal was to involve students in hands-on activities that require higher-order thinking skills, and also enable them to express their findings clearly in writing. The activities in this book are designed to do just that. Many of them require students to investigate and research a subject before creating the project that follows. By actively participating in each task, not only do students better remember what they have studied, but they also develop a clearer understanding of the concepts involved.

Today there are more commercially produced materials on the market that support Ohio's proficiency testing. However, we feel that the ideas and activities presented in this book will serve as a useful tool to assist any teacher working in grades 4–8. As you will see, these activities not only involve students in their own learning, but they also help children to read with greater skill and accuracy, and to write and think more critically.

Since we first began presenting these ideas in workshops around our area, we have had numerous requests from around the state to give additional workshops on hands-on social studies. We're happy now to be able to share these ideas with even more teachers through this book.

SUPPLY LIST

You may want to have the following supplies available for the activities in this book:

Scissors

Glue sticks

Paper—variety of sizes, kinds, and colors

Stapler and staples

Crayons or markers

Pencils

Yarn or string

Bulletin-board or butcher paper

Metal rings

Paper plates

Paper fasteners

Envelopes of various sizes

Calendar and magazine pictures

Map and Geography Activities

1 Identifying Landforms and Bodies of Water

Sometimes children have difficulty making the connection between physical features as they appear in the real world and those same features as they are shown on a flat, one-dimensional map. This activity is intended to help your students visualize what landforms and bodies of water look like. It can be used to help students locate specific places as close as in your own neighborhood or as distant as across the globe.

MATERIALS

Calendar or magazine pictures of landforms and bodies of water, several physical maps, construction paper, glue sticks

WHAT TO DO

Glue calendar or magazine pictures of landforms and bodies of water onto pieces of construction paper. Attach a description of the picture and its location on the back. Then cover the description with a flap so that students cannot readily see the answer. When you have finished, show each picture to the whole class. Ask students if they can locate it on a physical map. Next, organize the class into small groups or have them work in pairs (depending on how many physical maps or atlases are available). After distributing the pictures to each group, instruct them to record their findings to share with their classmates.

(Teacher Tip) I use only pictures of areas that I know the exact location of. Then I can identify a specific place on the map after students have made their guesses. Encourage older students to provide exact locations in latitude and longitude.

OTHER IDEAS

Let students find pictures of landforms and bodies of water to make their own set of cards.

2 Landforms and Bodies of Water Envelope Books

You can use this activity to expand upon what students have already learned about landforms and bodies of water. It should help them recall in a fun way the various physical features that are shown on a map.

MATERIALS

Copies of page 21 (landforms and bodies of water), business-size envelopes, index cards or construction paper, scissors, pencils, crayons or markers, magazines, old calendars, postcards, paper fasteners or stapler, and glue sticks

WHAT TO DO

Tell students to look through old magazines, books, calendars, postcards, and copies of page 21 to find pictures of landforms and bodies of water. After selecting several pictures, they should glue them to index cards or to small pieces of index card-size construction paper. On the back of the each card, they need to describe the landform or body of water and its exact location if they can determine that information. Instruct students to place each card inside an envelope and write

down three clues about the picture on the outside. This becomes their Riddle Book about Landforms and Bodies of Water. Encourage students to share their work with the rest of the class.

(Teacher Tip) You may want to use larger envelopes (5-by-8 or 9-by-12) to accommodate larger pictures.

3 Latitude and Longitude Game

This activity is designed to help students understand and use latitude and longitude. But, as you will see, it turns an often confusing concept into a fun-filled game.

MATERIALS

Index cards, markers

WHAT TO DO

On one set of index cards, write the names of either a city and state, or city and country (see the list on the next page). On another set of cards, write the latitude and longitude of each of these places. Then distribute the cards to the class. The students who receive the city cards need to figure out the latitude and longitude of their location. The students who receive the latitude and longitude cards need to locate the corresponding city and state or city and country. When they have collected the information they need, tell students to find the classmate who has either their city or their latitude and longitude.

UNITED STATES

New York City, New York	43° N & 78° W
Washington, D.C.	39° N & 77° W
Columbus, Ohio	40° N & 83° W
Detroit, Michigan	42° N & 83° W
Los Angeles, California	34° N & 118° W
Dallas, Texas	33° N & 97° W
Miami, Florida	26° N & 80° W
New Orleans, Louisiana	30° N & 90° W
Chattanooga, Tennessee	34° N & 85° W
Denver, Colorado	40° N & 105° W
Charleston, West Virginia	38° N & 82° W
Charleston, South Carolina	33° N & 80° W
Carson City, Nevada	39° N & 120° W
Boston, Massachusetts	42° N & 71° W
St. Louis, Missouri	39° N & 90° W

WORLD

Paris, France	49° N & 2° E
Melbourne, Australia	38° S & 145° E
London, England	52° N & 0°
Moscow, Russia	56° N & 38° E
Jerusalem, Israel	32° N & 35° E
Cairo, Egypt	30° N & 31° E
Rio de Janeiro, Brazil	23° S & 43° W
Baghdad, Iraq	33° N & 44° E
New Delhi, India	28° N & 77° E
Beijing, China	40° N & 116° E
Manila, Philippines	14° N & 121° E
Madrid, Spain	40° N & 4° W
Cape Town, South Africa	34° S & 18° E
Kinshasa, Zaire	4° S & 15° E
Nairobi, Kenya	1° S & 37° E

(Teacher Tip) A good follow-up activity is to have students locate different cities and states and their latitude and longitude.

4 Map Puzzles

This activity is designed to give students additional practice in working with maps. Most children will not pass up the opportunity to put together a puzzle.

MATERIALS

Old maps such as those from the American Automobile Association, local hotels and motels, and *National Geographic* magazine; a laminator

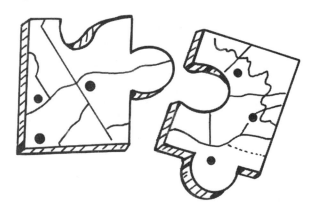

WHAT TO DO

These maps should be laminated and cut into puzzle-shaped pieces. Place them in a center area so that students can put the map pieces back together.

(Teacher Tip) As an extension activity, distribute the puzzle pieces to the class and ask students questions about the items they are holding. For example:

Who has a piece with a river on it?

Who has a mountain on his or her piece?

Who has a large city on his or her map? A small city? A landmark? A point of interest?

Tell me something that is on your puzzle piece.

5 Folding Maps

This activity should help students grasp the idea of the relative size of different places shown on a map, as well as the relationships between these places. Students can work in small groups to research and create their own maps.

MATERIALS

Bulletin-board or butcher paper, scissors, and pencils, crayons, or markers. (For this activity use only markers that do not bleed through the paper. Crayons are a better choice.)

WHAT TO DO

Students need to fold a large piece of paper in half four times. When they have folded down to the smallest section, they should draw the approximate shape of their city or town and label it. Then have students open to the next size and draw a map of their state. Tell them to continue by unfolding the paper to the next size and drawing a map of their country. Ask the children to open to the next size and draw a map of the continent they live on (or students might draw the Western

Hemisphere). Finally, instruct them to completely open up the paper and draw a map of the world. Students should make each map as large as its designated section. Encourage students to include illustrations and landmarks on each map.

   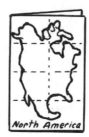 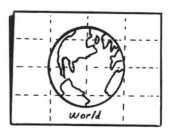

(Teacher Tip) You will probably want to move desks and tables out of the way so that students have room to work on the floor for this activity. You will need a variety of maps and atlases for students to use when they draw their maps.

OTHER IDEAS

Students who are studying their state could adapt this activity to include the following: city, county, state, surrounding states, and the United States.

6 Travel Brochure Maps

Have you ever wondered what to do with all those rumpled, misfolded road maps you collect while traveling? Well, here is one solution. This activity will not only give students practice reading road maps and finding various locations, it will also give them experience using different kinds of maps that show only a limited geographical area.

MATERIALS

Travel brochures and maps

WHAT TO DO

After showing students a large city map, make up a series of questions that ask them how to get from one place to another. See the box on the next page for some sample questions using a map of Chicago, Illinois.

(Teacher Tip) Encourage students to make up their own directions and quiz one another. You will probably want to laminate the map as well as your set of directions.

OTHER IDEAS

Visit nearby hotels and motels to pick up travel brochures and local maps that can be used with this activity.

7 Map Study Through Literature

There is nothing like an adventure story or spine-tingling tale to spark an interest in unknown people and places. The library is filled with books designed to draw children into a world of far-away lands and the people who live there.

MATERIALS

Several literature books, a large map for the bulletin board, yarn, reduced-size copies of the covers of books used

WHAT TO DO

Select several fictional stories from around the world. Then copy the cover of each book and reduce its size. Have students locate the origin of the story on a large map of the world. Then place the reduced copy of the book on the bulletin board outside the map. Ask students to attach one end of the yarn to the book and the other end to the map at the book's location. Encourage students to discuss the culture of each country that is identified. This can be either a year-long or a short-term project. Or it can become a permanent bulletin-board display.

8 Cinderella Literature

The story of Cinderella, with her grumpy, unattractive stepsisters and the debonair Prince Charming, has long fascinated children in all parts of the world. Exploit this interest to have students undertake a unique type of map and culture study.

MATERIALS

Different versions of *Cinderella* from around the world, a large map for the bulletin board, yarn, reduced-size copies of the books used

WHAT TO DO

Use the *Cinderella* literature as a vehicle for having students begin a map and culture study. Each version of the story in some way reflects the culture of the country represented. After reading the various books with the class, copy the covers and reduce their size. Then ask students to place the copied books on the bulletin board around a map of the world. Tell them to attach the book to its place of origin with a piece of yarn.

(Teacher Tip) Either make colored copies of the book covers or let students decorate them to make a more inviting display.

9 Literature and Map Study

Studying maps in conjunction with reading literature is an enjoyable way to learn about the world. Before beginning this activity, encourage your students to discuss any books they have read that focus on distant or exotic places.

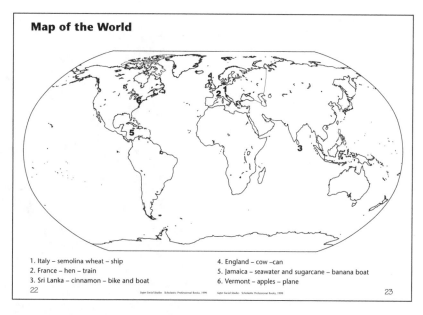

Map of the World

1. Italy – semolina wheat – ship
2. France – hen – train
3. Sri Lanka – cinnamon – bike and boat
4. England – cow –can
5. Jamaica – seawater and sugarcane – banana boat
6. Vermont – apples – plane

22   *Super Social Studies Scholastic Professional Books, 1999*   *Super Social Studies Scholastic Professional Books, 1999*   23

MATERIALS

Copies of pages 22–23, pencils, crayons or markers, and several works of fiction, as well as copies of *How to Make an Apple Pie and See the World* by Marjorie Priceman.

WHAT TO DO

Have students read *How to Make an Apple Pie and See the World* by Marjorie Priceman. Then initiate a discussion about all the places described in the story and the kinds of transportation used. Give students copies of pages 22–23 and let them label the map with the various sites mentioned in the book.

(Teacher Tip) Other books that can be used to do a map study include:

Everybody Eats Rice by Norah Dooley

A My Name is Alice by Jane Bayer

A Very Important Day by Maggie Rugg Herold

10 Book Maps

This activity can be done with either chapter or picture books. While using your social studies textbook will encourage students to review what they have learned, using fictional stories instead will force them to be more creative. After the selection has been chosen, students are asked to draw or paint whatever images come to mind. This is a good way to check reading comprehension as well as to help students form correct visualizations.

MATERIALS

Drawing paper, pencils, paints, crayons or markers, a book or literature selection

WHAT TO DO

After students have read the selection that has been chosen or have listened to it being read, tell them to draw whatever images the reading conjures up. Then instruct them to draw an imaginary map of the book's setting. The map can be of either one part of the selection or the setting as a whole.

(Teacher Tip)

Display finished maps on the class bulletin board or in the hallway.

11 Cookie Maps

Throughout our nation's history, people have established new settlements along the shores of rivers and lakes or accessible to natural harbors. This activity will help students understand the importance of water in the development of new cities and towns.

MATERIALS

State-shaped cookie cutter, sugar cookie dough, blue icing gel, mini chocolate chips, transparency of state (outline), and transparency markers

WHAT TO DO

Give each student a state cookie, blue icing gel, and some mini chocolate chips. Using the overhead projector, help students put several important rivers on their cookie with the icing gel. Next, instruct them to place the chocolate chips on the cookie to indicate major cities and towns. Be sure to use cities that are located along rivers. When this part of the activity is completed, students will usually say, "Gee, all of these cities are situated near rivers." This is your lead into a class discussion about the importance of water in the development of new communities.

(Teacher Tip) If you cannot locate a cookie cutter of your state, give students a pattern for them to trace and cut out (see pages 24–26). Then complete the same activity using crayons or markers and small stickers for the cities. Encourage students to read any of the following books:

A River Ran Wild by Lynne Cherry

Flood by Mary Calhoun

Letting Swift River Go by Jane Yolen

Three Days on a River in a Red Canoe by Vera B. Williams

Where the River Begins by Thomas Locker

12 Scrambled State Pictures

This fun activity will help your students learn about the 50 states.

MATERIALS

Copy of pages 24–26, paper, glue, and pens, pencils, or markers

WHAT TO DO

Instruct each student to use a copy of pages 24–26 to make his or her own special picture. First have the children cut out the states they want to include and place them on a sheet of paper. Each state may be used only once. When they have finished arranging the states to form a picture, students should color in their creations. Remind them to provide an imaginative title or caption. Finally, tell students to make a list of all the states they used in their picture.

(Teacher Tip) Encourage students to look up the name of the capital city of each state included in their creation.

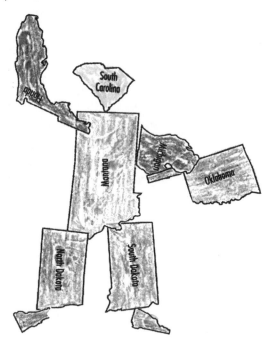

OTHER IDEAS

Hang the finished pictures on the bulletin board or in the hallway. All completed artwork could be collected to make a class book of our scrambled 50 states. You may want to have on hand the book *The Scrambled States of America* by Laurie Keller.

13 Geography and Research

Students will need to research the origins of different types of foods to complete this activity. Most children are surprised to discover where many of their favorite foods originated.

MATERIALS

A large map for the bulletin board, yarn or string, and cards showing different kinds of food

WHAT TO DO

After students have labeled each food card with its name, have them research the part of the world where it originated. Then have them position all the cards on the bulletin board around the outside of a large world map. Using a piece of string, they should connect each food card to the country of its origin.

14 Famous Names Around the World

As students do this fun activity they will be learning about the names and locations of countries around the world.

MATERIALS

Copy of page 27 and a world map or atlas

WHAT TO DO

First organize the class into small groups or have students work in pairs. Give each group a copy of page 27 and a world map or atlas. Then tell students that they need to find the name of a country that contains one of the boys' or girls' names on their list. For example, for "Mark," they might select the country Denmark. When students are done, post their lists around the classroom.

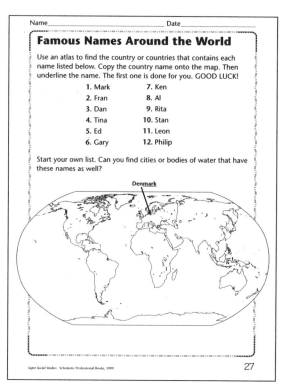

Famous Names Around the World

Use an atlas to find the country or countries that contains each name listed below. Copy the country name onto the map. Then underline the name. The first one is done for you. GOOD LUCK!

1. Mark	7. Ken
2. Fran	8. Al
3. Dan	9. Rita
4. Tina	10. Stan
5. Ed	11. Leon
6. Gary	12. Philip

Start your own list. Can you find cities or bodies of water that have these names as well?

Denmark

Super Social Studies Scholastic Professional Books, 1999

27

Teacher Tip Encourage students to put additional names on the list.

ANSWER KEY: Famous Names Around the World

1. Denmark
2. France
3. Sudan
4. Argentina
5. Sweden, United States
6. Hungary
7. Kenya
8. Malaysia, Mali, Portugal, Somalia, Algeria, Australia, Central African Republic, El Salvador, Guatemala, Italy
9. Mauritania, Great Britain
10. Pakistan, Afghanistan
11. Sierra Leone
12. Philippines

OTHER IDEAS

The name search could be limited to a specific continent, country, or state. Or it could be restricted to only cities or bodies of water.

15 Continent Envelopes

For this activity, students use a series of clues to determine which of the seven continents is being described. You should vary the difficulty of the clues depending on the grade you are teaching.

MATERIALS

Copy of page 28, seven large envelopes, pictures or maps of every continent, metal rings, glue

WHAT TO DO

Each picture or map of the seven continents should be placed inside its own envelope. After writing down three clues about each continent on a piece of paper (below), glue the clues to the front of the envelope. Then punch a hole in the corner of the envelopes and use a metal ring to keep them all together. For their part, students need to read the clues and decide which continent is hidden inside.

(Teacher Tip) Encourage students to research each continent and generate their own clues. They can use the graphic organizer on page 28 to gather research about their continent. Some of your students may want to write summaries or reports about the information they have collected.

Laminating the envelopes will make them sturdier and last longer.

SAMPLE CLUES FOR THE CONTINENTS

South America
1. This continent has mountain ranges and waterfalls.
2. It also has tropical rain forests.
3. Several countries on this continent export coffee, sugarcane, cacao, and bananas.

North America
1. This continent is the third largest landmass in the world.
2. Its early inhabitants crossed over a land bridge from Siberia about 20,000 years ago.
3. This continent grows most of the world's food.

Europe
1. Many social, economic, and political ideas originated on this continent.
2. It was the birthplace of the Industrial Revolution.
3. It has good supplies of coal and iron ore.

Australia
1. This is the smallest continent in the world.
2. It is surrounded by the Indian and Pacific oceans.
3. Many unusual animals live here that are found nowhere else in the world.

Asia
1. This is the largest continent in the world.
2. It has the largest population.
3. The principal crop grown here is rice.

Antarctica
1. This continent is located in the southernmost part of the world.
2. It is covered with ice and snow and has the coldest climate on earth.
3. No permanent residents live here.

Africa
1. This is the second largest continent.
2. It is located in all four hemispheres.
3. The longest river in the world flows through this landmass.

16 Interdependence of World Trade

This activity is designed to help students discover where various items found around the classroom and at home are made. It will demonstrate how much American consumers depend upon products manufactured all around the world.

MATERIALS

World map, pushpins or stickers, small stick-on notes, poster board

WHAT TO DO

Have students check the labels on their clothing, backpacks, shoes, and coats for the country where each product was made. They can use a pushpin or sticker to indicate on the map where the items were produced. After students have located each product on the map, initiate a discussion about their findings. Ask if there is a pattern to the pushpins or stickers. Then have the class discuss the significance of the pattern.

As a follow-up homework assignment, have students make a list of ten items found at home and tell where they were made. The next day ask students to write the name of each item and its place of origin on individual stick-on notes. Then instruct them to make a bar graph based on their findings. The countries should be listed along the horizontal axis with the stick-on notes positioned above the correct country.

(Teacher Tip) Use this activity to stimulate a discussion about world trade and the countries that appear to dominate the marketplace today. Ask students many *why* questions during this activity.

17 Export Game

This is another activity to help students better understand the interdependence of world trade among nations today.

MATERIALS

Index cards, ball of yarn

WHAT TO DO

Give each student an index card with the name of a country written on it. Students then need to spend some time researching that country's major imports and exports. After they have completed their research, instruct the children to list several of the imports and exports on their cards.

Next instruct students to punch two holes in their cards, tie a piece of yarn to each end, and place the completed sign around their necks. With the class standing in a circle, hand the ball of yarn to one student. That child holds on to one end of the yarn and tosses the ball to a classmate whose country exports a product needed by the first country. The game continues around the circle. The yarn may be passed to several of the same countries many times because other nations need their exports. An example might be to start with the United States tossing the yarn to Saudi Arabia for its oil; Saudi Arabia tosses to Canada for its automobiles; Canada then tosses to Japan for its electronic equipment, and so forth.

(Teacher Tip) Remind the class that some countries that do not have important exports may be dominant in the world marketplace because of their abundant labor supply.

Name_____ Date_____

Map of the World

Super Social Studies Scholastic Professional Books, 1999

Name________________________________ Date____________________

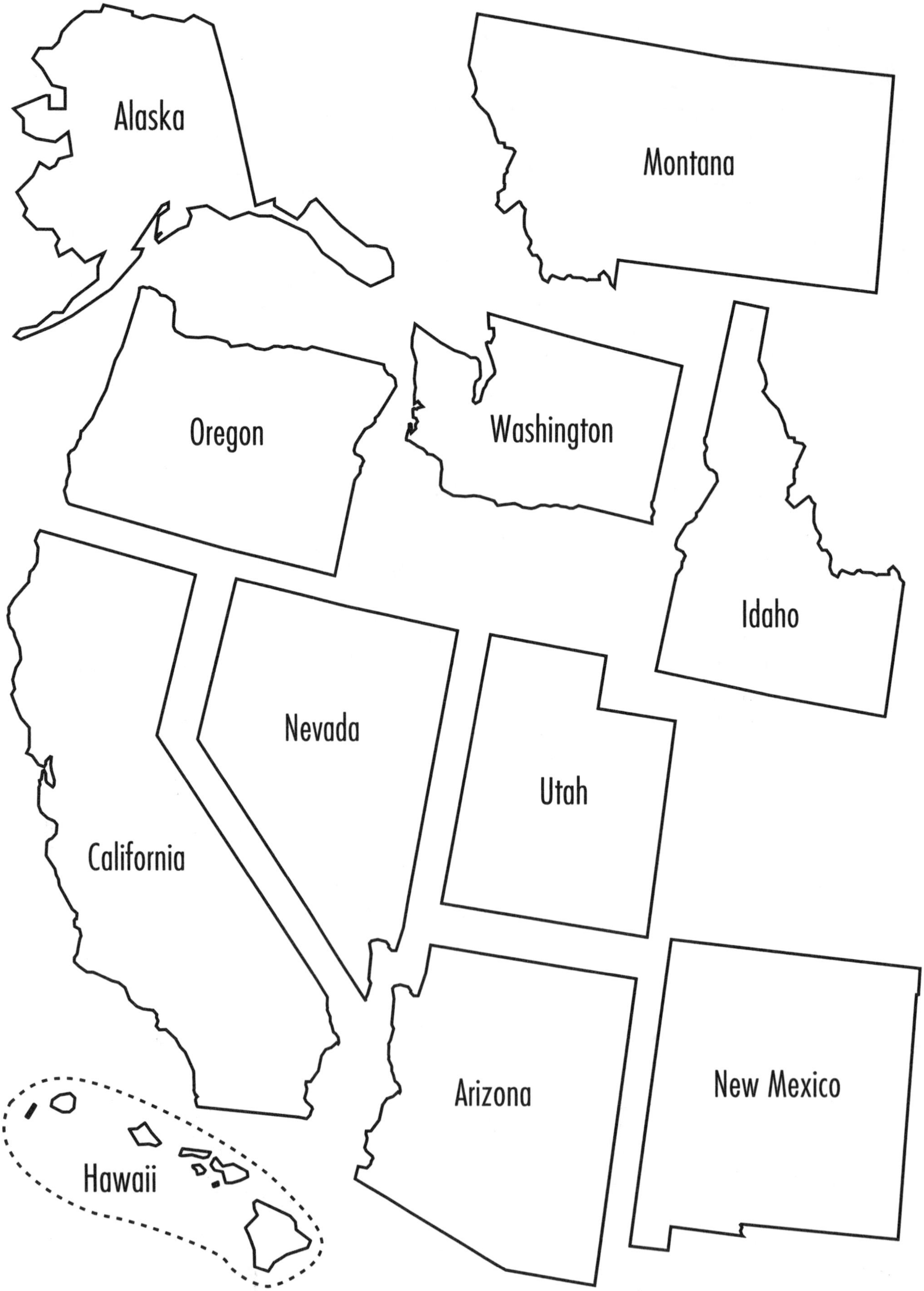
Alaska
Montana
Oregon
Washington
Idaho
Nevada
Utah
California
Arizona
New Mexico
Hawaii

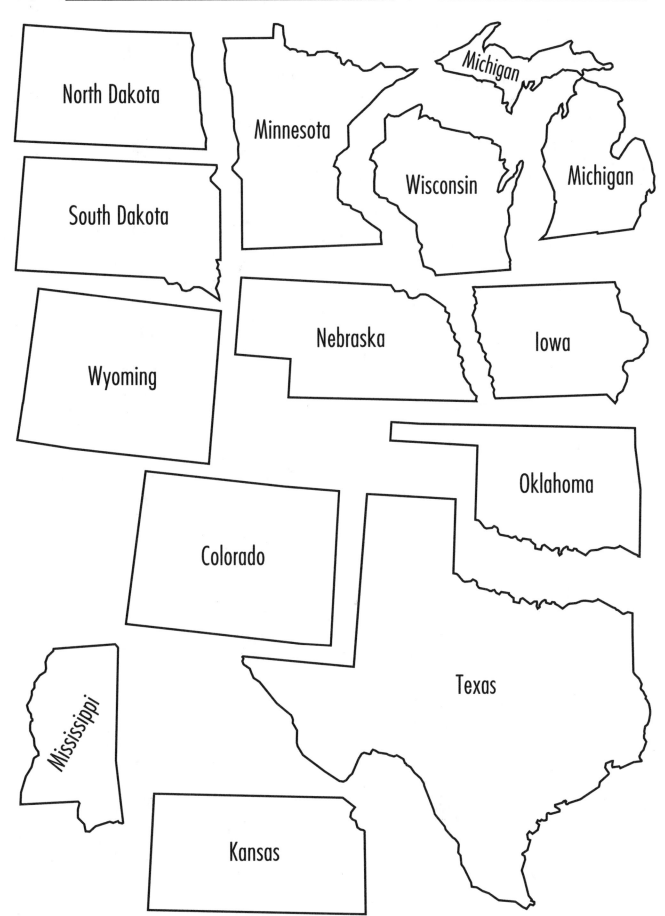

North Dakota

Minnesota

Michigan

Wisconsin

Michigan

South Dakota

Wyoming

Nebraska

Iowa

Oklahoma

Colorado

Texas

Mississippi

Kansas

Super Social Studies Scholastic Professional Books, 1999

Famous Names Around the World

Use an atlas to find the country or countries that contains each name listed below. Copy the country name onto the map. Then underline the name. The first one is done for you. GOOD LUCK!

1. Mark		**7.** Ken	
2. Fran		**8.** Al	
3. Dan		**9.** Rita	
4. Tina		**10.** Stan	
5. Ed		**11.** Leon	
6. Gary		**12.** Philip	

Start your own list. Can you find cities or bodies of water that have these names as well?

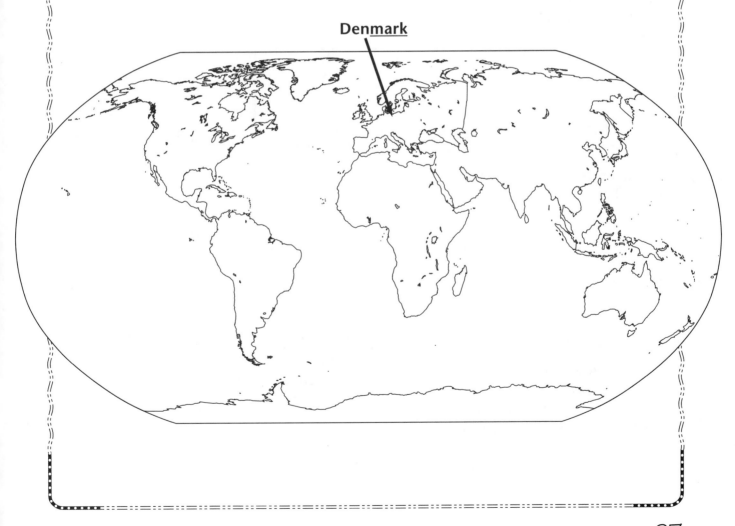

Denmark

Find Out More About This Continent

Research one of the continents of the world to uncover the information needed to answer the following questions. Then write a report about your findings.

8.
Would you like to visit this continent? Why or why not?

9.
Would you like to live on this continent? Why or why not?

1.
What is the climate like there?

7.
Does this continent have navigable waterways? If yes, name one.

_____
Name of the Continent

2.
Describe the major landforms found on this continent.

6.
What kinds of animals live there?

3.
What kinds of crops are grown there?

5.
How many countries are included within this continent? Name the largest country.

4.
Name the oceans that touch this continent.

28

Timeline Activities

18 Human Timeline

This activity will help students better understand time relationships by having them put themselves in order according to their birthdays.

MATERIALS

Index card, markers

WHAT TO DO

Ask students to write down the day, month, and year on which they were born. Then have them arrange themselves into a human timeline according to the date of their birth. As an extension activity, pass out cards with the name and birthday of several key people that the class has been studying. Tell students to form a timeline based on the date of birth of these individuals.

OTHER IDEAS

Have students form several groups to research a particular topic. When they have finished, each group should form a human timeline based on the events that occurred during the period being studied.

19 Pocket Chart Timeline

This activity provides yet another way to help students understand the relationship between time and events.

MATERIALS

Index cards, pencils, and crayons or markers.

WHAT TO DO

On two sets of index cards, write down several important events and the dates on which they occurred. Then have students place each date card across from the corresponding event.

Teacher Tip This activity can be set up in a center so that students can place the cards in the appropriate pockets. It should serve as a good reinforcement or retesting activity. You might want to change the events and the corresponding dates every couple of weeks as your social studies curriculum progresses.

20 Paper Chain Timeline

Paper chain timelines help students envision the sequence of major historical events. They also help children to better understand the relationship between time and events in history.

MATERIALS

Colored paper, scissors, glue sticks or stapler, pencils, crayons or markers, and pieces of string or yarn

WHAT TO DO

Have students cut paper into strips to create a paper chain. Periods of time such as decades and centuries should be different colors. Write the date or time period on each colored section of the paper chain. Then, on separate pieces of paper, have students list historical events that occurred during each time frame and attach them to the chain with yarn or string.

Teacher Tip

Completed paper chains can be hung in the classroom or in the hallway.

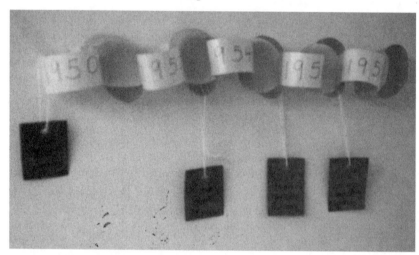

21 Step Book Timeline

This activity can be used with a limited number of dates taken from either an historical period or an individual's life.

MATERIALS

Copies of pages 33–34, paper, scissors, stapler, pencils, and crayons or markers

WHAT TO DO

Help children make individual step books by following the instructions on pages 33–34. After they staple the pages, they will need to label several periods of time in consecutive order on the borders. For each time period, they should add an illustration and a short paragraph telling about an event that took place during that time period.

(Teacher Tip) Display the finished step books in the classroom or in the hallway.

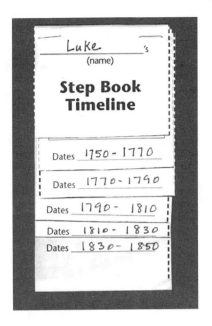

22 Accordion Timeline

In this activity, students make a timeline that they can continue to add to as they study a time period or a person's life.

MATERIALS

Copy of page 35, construction paper, scissors, glue sticks or stapler, pencils, and crayons or markers

WHAT TO DO

Ask students to cut the page as indicated. They should tape the four sections together. (They can add more sections if they wish.) They should glue or staple both ends to covers (cut to size) made from construction paper. Encourage students to illustrate the cover creatively and then label it. Then have them label each accordion page of the timeline with a date or time period and list several important events that occurred then.

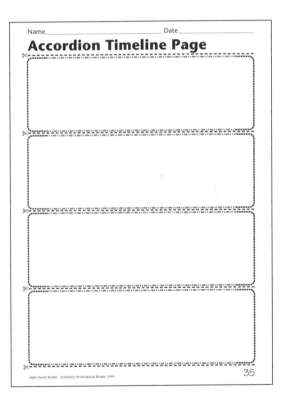

(Teacher Tip) An accordion timeline might be used to chronicle school events from September to June. Then the children will have a record of their activities throughout the current school year. In this way, the timeline becomes a personal record for students to contribute to and share.

23 Famous Person Timeline

This activity provides students with the unique opportunity to combine role playing with learning about the sequence of events as they appear on a timeline.

MATERIALS

Appropriate costumes for several famous people, material for a timeline (bulletin-board paper), scissors, pencils, and crayons or markers

WHAT TO DO

After students have chosen a famous person to dramatize, they need to memorize about two to three minutes worth of information about that individual. When they are ready to share what they have learned, move to a larger room or push the classroom furniture out of the way. Next put a timeline on the wall or on the floor and have the students, in costume, stand completely still along the dates on the timeline when their key figure lived. Place a sticker or mark on each child's hand. When the sticker or mark is pressed, that child "comes to life" and tells about the famous person that he or she is dressed as. Invite other classes and parents to view this unique dramatization.

(Teacher Tip) You may need to help some students write their script. Also, it is important to provide some guidelines and suggestions on what should be included about each person. At least one interesting or funny incident should be dramatized.

24 Filmstrip Timeline

This activity lets students create a special timeline that resembles a roll of film. The children will enjoy covering each white block with important dates, facts, and illustrations.

MATERIALS

Copy of page 36, pencils, crayons or markers, scissors, and glue sticks or stapler

WHAT TO DO

After students have researched information for their timeline, give them copies of page 36. Have them cut the segments apart. Ask them to write and illustrate several events for their timelines as if each event were a segment of a filmstrip. Students will need to glue or staple together a few sections of film to make one continuous roll. When they have completed their timeline information, the children can wind the strip up like a roll of film.

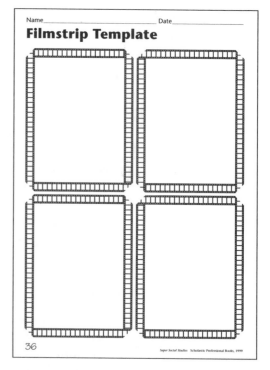

Name_____ Date_____

Filmstrip Template

36

Super Social Studies Scholastic Professional Books, 1999

Timeline Step Book

Cut along the dashed lines and fold along the solid lines to make a timeline step book.

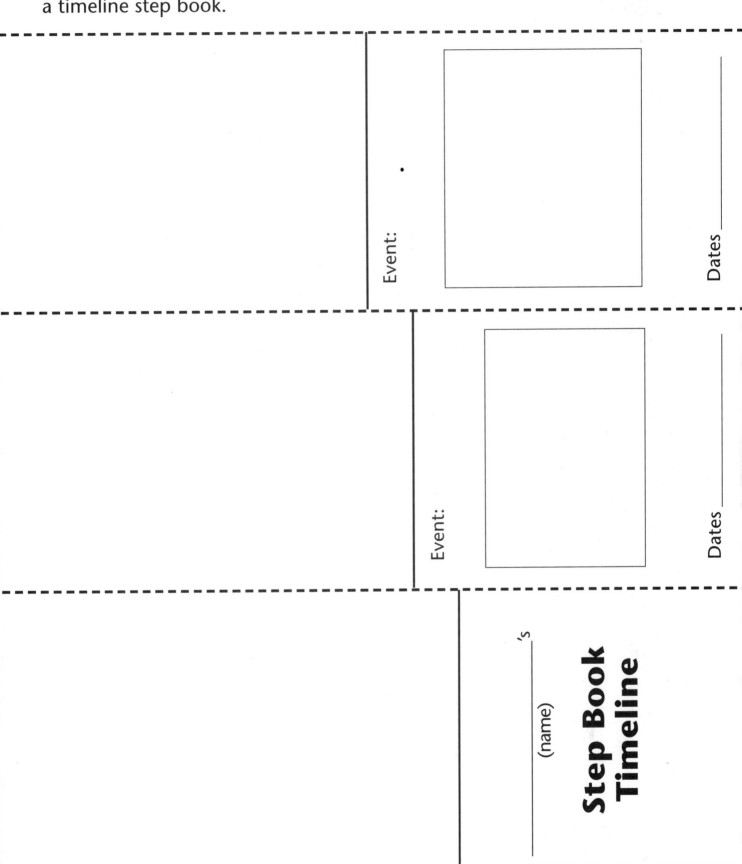

Event:

Dates _____

Event:

Dates _____

_____'s

(name)

Step Book Timeline

Super Social Studies   Scholastic Professional Books, 1999

Timeline Step Book

Cut along the dashed lines and fold along the solid lines to make a step book timeline.

Event:

Dates

Event:

Dates

Event:

Dates

Super Social Studies Scholastic Professional Books, 1999

Name_____ Date_____

Accordion Timeline

Super Social Studies   Scholastic Professional Books, 1999

Name_____ Date_____

Filmstrip Template

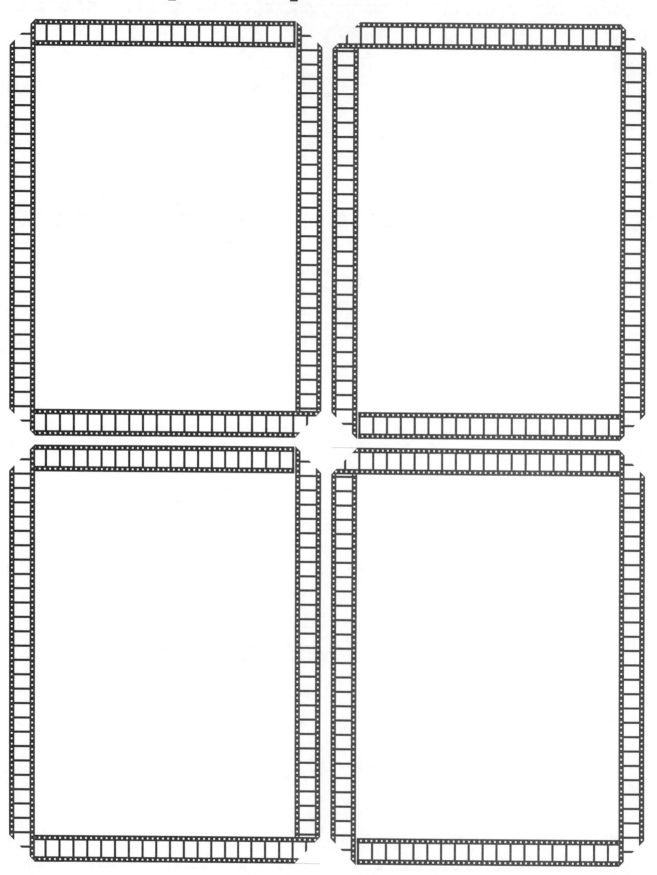

36

Super Social Studies   Scholastic Professional Books, 1999

Research and Reporting Activities

25 Let's Play Concentration

This activity should help make remembering important new people and places a lot more enjoyable and hopefully a little bit easier.

MATERIALS

Poster-board paper, construction paper, index cards, scissors, glue, self-sticking Velcro, and markers or a computer printout

WHAT TO DO

First glue 12 to 16 flaps of construction paper to the poster board and number the flaps. Then select about six or eight important facts from the social studies topic that your class is currently studying. These will need to be written on index cards. The answers should be written out on the remaining six or eight cards. For example, include the card, Benjamin Franklin, with the matching card, Discovered Electricity. You might find it easier to use a computer to print out the questions as well as the answers. Finally, Velcro the index cards to the poster board under the flaps.

HOW TO PLAY: Student A lifts up two flaps. If he or she makes a match, the cards should be removed from the poster board. If not, the student needs to remember which flaps were chosen. Student B continues by lifting two more flaps. The student with the most matches wins. It might be helpful to place a paper clip on the flaps when a match has been made. To help preserve the game, the board should be laminated.

GAME VARIATION: When a match is made, the student has to give additional information about the topic. For example, Benjamin Franklin wrote *Poor Richard's Almanac.*

(Teacher Tip) After a lesson, have each student make two cards that can be used with the Concentration game. This way, the game will be constantly changing while students become active participants in the learning process.

26 State Bookmarks

These bookmarks are a hands-on way for students to learn facts about individual states.

MATERIALS

Copies of pages 24–26 and 57, oaktag, scissors, glue, paper fasteners

WHAT TO DO

Encourage students to decide which state they wish to research. Provide them with the outline of that state (found on pages 24–26) and the bookmark reproducible (page 57). Suggest that they use textbooks, encyclopedias, reference books, and the Internet to complete the bookmarks. Also ask them to cut out the state they've chosen, and to add as many labels as possible to the map. They should, however, be sure to include the state capital. Have them glue the bookmark and the state to a sheet of oaktag (or a recycled folder) as shown in the illustration (left). The state outline should be glued so it forms the top of the bookmark. You may need to enlarge the state outline. Have children then cut out the bookmark. Suggest that they add an interesting fact or tell about a famous person from the state on the reverse side of the bookmark. If possible, laminate the bookmarks so they remain durable.

You may want to have students combine the bookmarks into region books. Punch a hole in the bottom of the bookmarks and attach them with a paper fastener.

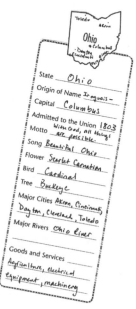

27 Calendar State Scrapbooks

Sometimes students who have not had the opportunity to travel across their state do not appreciate its tremendous diversity. Whether you live on the east coast, the west coast, or somewhere in between, this scrapbook activity will help give students some idea of how life varies from one part of their state to the other.

MATERIALS

State calendars, large sheets of construction paper, an outline map of your state

WHAT TO DO

Glue the calendar pictures to large pieces of colored construction paper. With the help of the class, begin locating each picture on the state outline map. Then label the page with the picture's location as well as its exact latitude and longitude (if appropriate for your grade). When the class has finished, you might want to laminate the pages. The completed book can be placed in a center area to be used throughout the year.

(Teacher Tip) Check discount stores or bookshops for outdated calendars. Often they can be purchased for less than half price.

28 Paper-Plate Picture Frames

Using paper plates, this activity gives students the opportunity both to draw pictures of what they have been studying and to display these drawings in an unusual way.

MATERIALS

White paper plates, used laminating film or plastic wrap, scissors, stapler, pens, pencils, markers, paper

WHAT TO DO

First, have your students draw and color a picture on a white paper plate (for example, a landform such as a mountain or valley). Then have them cut a piece of used laminating film or plastic wrap to fit over their drawing. The plastic needs to be stapled to the edge of the paper plate. For the next step, instruct your students to cut out the flat circular middle of a second plate, leaving only the outside edge. Then have them staple the second plate over their picture and plastic to form a frame. A description can be written on a piece of paper and glued to the back of the plate or stapled to the bottom edge of the picture frame.

OTHER IDEAS

Topics for picture frames might include any of the following: landforms and bodies of water, famous historical figures, and states and their symbols.

29 Four-Flap Books

These easy-to-make books are a great way to check your students' understanding of the main idea and supporting details of a particular social studies lesson. Any misunderstandings or unclear concepts can be clarified in a subsequent lesson.

MATERIALS

Copy of page 56, various sizes of paper, pens, pencils, markers

WHAT TO DO

Have students use the directions on page 56 for creating their four-flap book. After reading a lesson and discussing it, have them write a detail or fact you've discussed in the lesson on each of the four flaps. Have them write the main idea on the very last center section. Students can draw a picture to accompany each fact or detail on the reverse side of the flap.

Teacher Tip Save the books for different lessons for the class to use later as a lesson review.

OTHER IDEAS

You can use the same four-flap book format to have students write riddles about their lesson topics. Have them write a riddle on each flap, and the answer on the reverse side. This format is also a good way to review key social studies vocabulary, people, and places.

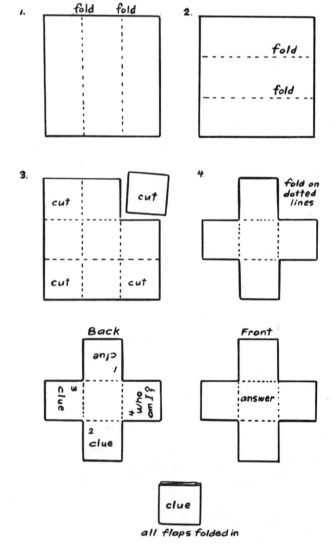

30 Step Book Ideas

Step books are easy for students to fold and can be adapted to many activities by adding or subtracting sheets of paper. This step-book project encourages students not only to research the life of a famous individual, but also to try thinking and feeling like that person. The activity will give students a better understanding of a well-known figure as they attempt to "become" someone famous.

MATERIALS

Copy of page 58, three pieces of paper for each student, stapler, pens, paper, markers

WHAT TO DO

Create a sample step book of a famous person that you admire. You will need to demonstrate to students how to fold the six flaps in a step book. Tell the class to label the steps with the following headings:

- ✛ person's name
- ✛ I live or lived
- ✛ I do or did
- ✛ I am
- ✛ I like or liked
- ✛ I wish or wished

Students need to complete the phrase on each step under the flap and illustrate it. The prompts on the steps can be adapted or adjusted according to the wishes of the students or the teacher. When they have completed their work, let students share their step books with the rest of the class.

(Teacher Tip) The step books can be used as part of a bulletin board display on famous people. This format helps students to better understand the point of view of the person they selected.

OTHER IDEAS

Step books can be cut into shapes that might represent an object related to that famous person. For example, Abraham Lincoln might be represented by a top hat; Johnny Appleseed, a pot; and Harriet Tubman, a knapsack.

Remind students to cut their step books into the shape of a top hat before they begin so that they won't cut off their writing or illustrations.

Step books that are based on a literature prompt are also useful in stimulating children's imaginations. Share Judith Viorst's poem, "If I Were in Charge of the World." Use the prompt "If I Were President...." and a copy of page 58. Then have students complete the following pattern:

(title step) If I Were President

- ✛ I would cancel....
- ✛ You wouldn't have....
- ✛ Would still be allowed to....
- ✛ There would be....
- ✛ And a person who....

Students could use the same format with any of the following topics: If I Were Governor, Mayor, Senator, Principal, etc. Other subjects might include: key vocabulary from a social studies lesson, historical events, landforms and bodies of water, map symbols, and major cities around the world.

31 Flip Books

Flip books can be adapted to fit the number of flip-up pages needed for a particular project. This adaptability gives students the freedom to organize their information or research in an interesting format.

MATERIALS

Three pieces of any size paper for each student, scissors, glue sticks, pencils, and crayons or markers

WHAT TO DO

When students have finished their research, they are ready to assemble this information into a flip book.

Give each student three pieces of paper. Then provide them with the following directions:

✛ Fold two sheets of paper in half the long way.

✛ Fold again into four equal sections.

✛ Open the paper and cut on each fold halfway up, resulting in four flips. The two pieces of paper will make eight flips.

✛ Glue the two pieces of paper onto the third sheet. One set of flips is on the front and one is on the back.

OTHER IDEAS

If the project requires many flips, this can be accomplished by cutting more and adding them to both sides of the third piece of paper. For example, if students were doing research on the members of the president's cabinet, they would need more than eight flips.

SUGGESTIONS FOR TOPICS

The following are possible topics that can be used to create flip books: the causes and effects of major historical events; various aspects of world trade; landforms and bodies of water; forms and branches of government; significant events of an era or period of time; key people involved in an historical event; information on a particular city, state, country, or continent; and factors of production (land, labor, capital, and entrepreneurship).

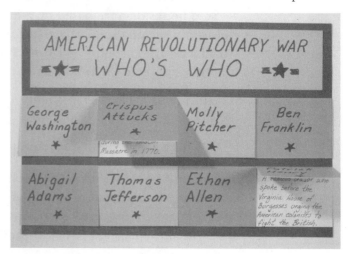

(32) Pop-up Books

Pop-up books are great to use as part of a collective project on a given topic. Each student can contribute a page to a class book on the subject or subjects being researched.

MATERIALS

Paper, scissors, pencils, and crayons or markers

WHAT TO DO

After the class has completed its research for the topic being studied, each student should create a page for the class book. Each page needs to include a title, a pop-up drawing, and a paragraph.

(Teacher Tip) Class books can be placed in a center area so students can read their pop-up books often.

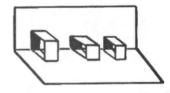

OTHER IDEAS

Students can work in cooperative groups on the topic "The Branches of Government," in order to create an original pop-up book. They may want to cut out information and pictures from newspapers and magazines. When each group has completed its book, it should share the finished product with the rest of the class.

SUGGESTIONS FOR TOPICS

The following are possible topics that can be used to create pop-up books: ABC's of a particular government, state, country, or continent; information about people, places, or events; and facts relating to consumers and producers, goods and services, and factors of production (land, labor, capital, and entrepreneurship).

33 ABC Research

An ABC activity based on a particular person, state, country, or event gives students a good opportunity to research a topic and be creative in their presentation of the material.

MATERIALS

Construction paper, paper, glue sticks, pencils, crayons or markers, research books, hole-punch, metal rings, paper fasteners, spiral rings, and string for binding

WHAT TO DO

Students need to research their topic in order to have enough information to use every letter of the alphabet. Each child can create his or her own ABC book or the

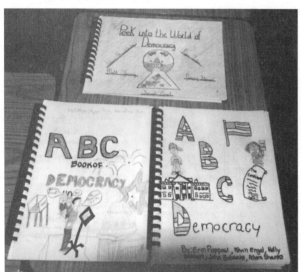

entire class can produce a book together. After students have written and illustrated each page, bind the book together using metal rings, paper fasteners, spiral rings, or string. Finally, hand out sheets of construction paper so that students can create front and back covers for their ABC books.

(Teacher Tip) When students are doing ABC research on a topic, it may be necessary to allow them to use a word with x in it for x and z in it for z. I find that if you do not allow these choices, students come up with some really silly words for x and z.

34 Trioramas

Many times it is difficult to collect enough boxes to make individual dioramas. But it is very easy and quick for students to make trioramas that display scenes from history or events in a person's life. They are also useful for showing the three branches of government as well as different forms of government such as monarchy, dictatorship, and democracy. Several trioramas can be glued or stapled together to create the project below. As they work through this activity, most students find history and government becoming more understandable as they transform often confusing ideas into concrete form.

MATERIALS

Copy of page 59, paper, scissors, glue or stapler, pencils, crayons or markers, and collected items for each individual triorama

WHAT TO DO

Have students follow the directions on page 59 to make the triorama shape. Ask each student to select a person or event that the class has been learning about as the subject of his or her project.

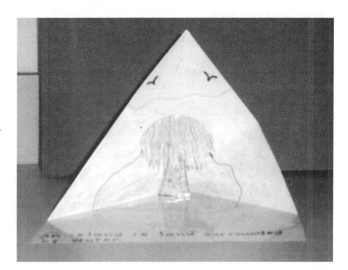

[Teacher Tip] Students may
want to collect things to put in
their triorama such as feathers,
egg cartons, craft sticks,
tongue depressors, stones, arti-
ficial flowers, and small toy animals and figures.

OTHER IDEAS

After students know how to
fold a triorama, they can use
bigger pieces of paper to make
even larger creations.

35 Wondercircles

This easy-to-make project results in an attractive display of student knowledge. Wondercircles
can be any size depending upon the topic. I have found that a plastic peanut-can lid makes a
good circle pattern and is easy to store. If you punch a hole in the lid and put it on a piece of
string or yarn, it can be hung up until needed again.

MATERIALS

Paper, scissors, pencils, crayons or markers, glue sticks, string or yarn, and plastic
straws or small sticks

WHAT TO DO

Ask students to trace and cut out five circles. Then have them write information on
each circle. (A list of possible topics is given below.) Students should fold each ring

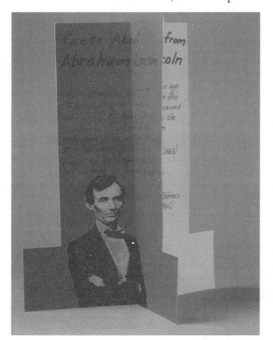

in half, with the writing on the inside (left to right and
right side up). Next, have them glue half of circle 1 to
half of circle 2, continuing to glue until the last circle
is attached to the first one, thus creating one large
ring. Finished wondercircles can be hung from a
string or glued to a small stick or straw. Wondercircles
will stand if the bottom of the circle is cut off.

[Teacher Tip] Wondercircles can be cut in various
shapes as long as the object is symmetrical. Christmas
trees, stars, kites, hearts, ovals, squares, triangles,
tulips, and hats all make decorative wondercircles.

OTHER IDEAS

There are many other topics for wondercircles. For
example, have students write down facts and draw pictures about any of the following: a famous person, cultural group, or historical event; a city, state, or coun-

45

try; vocabulary from a particular social studies lesson or historical novel; landforms and bodies of water; and factors of production. A wondercircle about a child's life might contain such information as:

1. How the child got to (insert appropriate town and state)
2. His or her name
3. Birthplace
4. Mother's name and birthplace
5. Father's name and birthplace

A wondercircle variation is a top hat that can be used in conjunction with research on a political leader or issue. Each hat might contain the following information:

1. Name of the candidate
2. Candidate's political party
3. Biographical information
4. Reasons for supporting the candidate
5. A political slogan or poster

Another possibility is a ballot question. In this case, have students do the following:

1. Briefly describe the question or issue.
2. State who would benefit from its passage.
3. Provide reasons for supporting the ballot issue.
4. Create a catchy slogan.
5. Design an attractive poster in support of the question or issue.

 # Trifold Activities

The trifold activities described below can be created in a variety of ways. They require students to research information and interpret that material in a meaningful way.

A literature trifold is an activity that has students interpret and illustrate a passage of historical writing.

MATERIALS

Paper, pencils, and crayons or markers

WHAT TO DO

Choose a literature selection. (Initially, I would use the same passage for the entire class.) Then have students follow the directions below:

- ✣ Fold the paper in thirds widthwise.
- ✣ On the top outside flap, write the title of the book or article.
- ✣ On the bottom outside flap, write the name of the author.
- ✣ On the top inside flap, copy an exact quote from the selection.
- ✣ In the middle section, illustrate the quotation.

✤ Finally, on the bottom inside flap, write about what you think the passage means.

(Teacher Tip) Collect the literature trifolds to display on a bulletin board. Or make a class collection of the trifolds by punching a hole in the corner of each one and tying them together or putting them on a metal ring.

37 More Trifold Topics

The paper used for these trifold activities should be folded lengthwise. As you can see, they ask students to write about and illustrate important people, places, and ideas.

MATERIALS

Paper, pencils, and crayons or markers

WHAT TO DO

After students have researched their topics and gathered the information needed, have them follow these instructions for the trifolds below:

STATE REPORT

✤ Outside flap—write the name of the state.

✤ First inside flap—include several important facts about the state.

✤ Second outside flap—write a summary about the state.

✤ Second inside map—draw a map.

✤ Third inside flap—choose one interesting fact or person from the state and write about it. Include a picture or drawing, if possible. This flap could also be a journal entry about someone such as an early immigrant to the state or a present-day resident.

✤ Back—list sources of information.

FAMOUS PERSON REPORT

✤ Outside flap—write the name of your famous person.

✤ First inside flap—include important facts about the person.

✤ Second inside flap—write a summary of the person, including a drawing or picture.

✤ Third inside flap—give three reasons for choosing this person and describe what you admire about his or her life.

✤ Back—list sources of information.

OTHER IDEAS

Other possible topics for trifolds include: cultural groups; countries or continents; periods of history; significant wars; the Industrial Revolution; the civil rights movement; exploration of the New World; factors of production; forms of government; and the three branches of government.

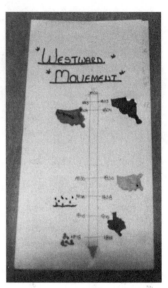

⟨38⟩ History Webs

This activity gives students an opportunity to depict the lifestyles and culture of a particular time period or movement in history.

MATERIALS

Drawing paper, pencils, and crayons or markers

WHAT TO DO

Have students divide the drawing paper into eight sections. (See the illustration below.) The space in the middle is for the title of the web. Each of the eight sections should depict scenes from the era or movement being studied in class. Students will need to research the topic being discussed to have a clear understanding of the issues involved.

Teacher Tip Have the children do a rough draft before starting on their final version. After the class has finished its history webs, you might want to create a bulletin-board display.

39 Shape Books

Compiling research in shape books provides a motivational boost for students.

MATERIALS

Construction paper, paper, glue, pens, pencils, markers, and stapler, or metal or spiral rings

WHAT TO DO

Draw (or have a student draw) a shape related to a topic you want the class to research. (See the list below for ideas.) Provide each student with a copy of the drawing. Ask them to find one fact about the topic, write it in the shape, and illustrate it. Have them cut out the shape. Trace and cut out the shape from construction paper for the cover. Compile every class member's page into a class book.

(Teacher Tip) Encourage students to write poems and draw illustrations related to your research topic.

OTHER IDEAS

Here's a list of simple shapes and related research topics:

- ⊕ **Eagle or flag**—American symbols
- ⊕ **Donkey or elephant**—political candidates/campaign issues
- ⊕ **Silhouette profile**—famous Americans
- ⊕ **Capitol building**—U.S. government
- ⊕ **Covered wagon**—pioneer experience

40 Significant Individuals

This activity will help students better understand some of the well-known people that fill the pages of their social studies textbook. It should help them appreciate that famous men and women have strengths as well as weaknesses. And, like the rest of us, they have to deal with real, everyday problems.

MATERIALS

Copy of page 60, paper, pencils, and pens

WHAT TO DO

After reading or studying about a key historical figure, students should use a copy of page 60 to record information about the individual they have selected. When their organizer is

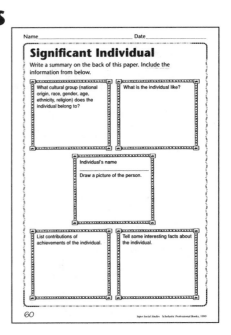

complete, have students write a brief summary using the facts and figures that they have compiled.

(Teacher Tip) Students can make a notebook or folder of famous people. This graphic organizer can be used any time students encounter information on a significant individual.

41 Accordion Snapshot Books

In this activity, students create a snapshot album of a significant individual. Like the project on page 49, it should help give children a better understanding of a well-known person.

MATERIALS

Copy of page 61, construction paper, scissors, glue sticks, pencils, and crayons or markers

WHAT TO DO

Over the course of the school year the class will probably read about several well-known historical figures. Have students select a famous person who, for one reason or another, piques their interest. Then ask them to illustrate and write captions for a variety of snapshots that capture highlights of that person's life. The completed snapshots should be cut out and taped together (accordion-style) in chronological order. Finally, students need to design a construction-paper cover to be attached to the folded snapshots.

42 Artifacts of the Rich and Famous

In this activity about famous people, students present an oral report, but in a very unique way. As part of their presentation, the children will display a series of artifacts that in some way represent the individual whom they have selected. In the process of picking out each one of these items, your students will gain a better understanding of a key historical figure.

MATERIALS

Items to be used as artifacts, a container to hold these items

WHAT TO DO

Students need to collect several items that are pertinent to the story of their famous person. Ask the children to give a report about the life and accomplishments of that person, explaining why they selected each one of the artifacts.

Example: Johnny Appleseed
1. A burlap bag or sack
2. Small animals
3. The Good Book
4. A small pot
5. An apple
6. Apple seeds

 Teacher Tip If students cannot find enough appropriate artifacts, they should draw or make what they need. But encourage them to be creative and find as many as they can.

43 Collect-All Drawer

This activity, which is similar to the one on page 50, provides students with yet another way to become better acquainted with a famous person. For this project the children will need to collect various items connected to the life and accomplishments of a well-known historical figure.

MATERIALS

A box lid, items that represent numerous famous people

WHAT TO DO

Use a box lid to serve as a collect-all drawer of a famous person. Students need to collect artifacts that might be found in that drawer. As they give their reports, students should explain why they chose each item for the drawer.

Example: Benjamin Franklin
1. Key
2. Glasses
3. Small kite
4. Piece of string
5. Piece of newspaper or almanac

Snapshot Books

Students can use this type of book to create an album about a famous person or historical event. By illustrating snapshots and writing captions, they can display their knowledge about any topic that the class is currently studying.

MATERIALS

Copy of page 61, construction paper, pencils, crayons or markers, hole-punch, rings, paper fasteners, or string

WHAT TO DO

Have students illustrate about six to eight snapshots that depict events in a particular person's life or period of history. Each drawing should be accompanied by an informative caption. Students cut out each snapshot, punch a hole in it, and use a metal ring, paper fastener, or string to bind the book together. Front and back covers can be made from construction paper.

(Teacher Tip) I have my students plan out and sketch their illustrations before using the actual snapshot pages.

Dramatizations of People or Historical Events

This is a wonderful activity for having your students dramatize a person's life or an event in history. By wearing authentic period dress and reciting appropriate lines, students feel that they are reliving part of our nation's history.

MATERIALS

Appropriate costumes, paper, pencils

WHAT TO DO

Students will need to research and write scripts in order to prepare for their skits. Having the class dressed in realistic costumes will help the audience better appreciate the people and events that are being dramatized. If

they prefer, students can pantomime rather than memorize their lines.

(Teacher Tip) Students might enjoy performing their skits for another class, parents, or the entire school.

46 Portrait Reports

As you will see, this activity is an oral report about a famous person.

MATERIALS
Old picture frames

WHAT TO DO

When students are ready to present their research about a well-known person, have them hold a picture frame and pretend to be the person they have selected.

Instruct students to be as animated as possible when giving their report. Not only is the picture frame a fun idea, but the very act of holding it may help relieve the jitters as the children stand up in front of the entire class.

(Teacher Tip) Students might enjoy dressing up as their famous people when presenting their oral reports.

47 Artifact Study

This activity will help students recognize and evaluate items from the past and give them a better understanding of what life was like during an earlier time. In conjunction with this activity, you might want to plan a field trip to an historical restoration in your area.

MATERIALS
Copy of page 62, collection of artifacts, pencils

WHAT TO DO
Organize students into groups or have them choose a partner. (The number of

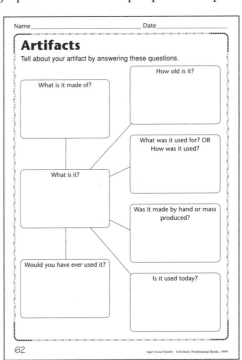

Name_____ Date_____

Artifacts
Tell about your artifact by answering these questions.

What is it made of?

How old is it?

What is it?

What was it used for? OR How was it used?

Was it made by hand or mass produced?

Would you have ever used it?

Is it used today?

Super Social Studies Scholastic Professional Books, 1999

groups will depend on how many artifacts are available.) Give each group a copy of page 62 as well as an artifact. Students need to answer the questions in each box about their particular object. Encourage each group to share its artifact with the rest of the class and describe what the group thinks it is. After everyone has finished, tell students what the item actually is.

(Teacher Tip) Over the years, I have collected interesting artifacts from flea markets and antiques shops. Students may have some items at home that they can bring in to share.

48 Factors of Production

Students often find it difficult to distinguish among the four factors of production. This activity should help them identify the different components—land, labor, capital, and entrepreneurship—that are needed to manufacture a product.

MATERIALS

Old magazines, poster board, construction paper, scissors, yarn, glue sticks, pencils, and crayons or markers

WHAT TO DO

Students should go through old magazines looking for pictures that illustrate the four factors of production. After they have selected several examples, have them cut out the pictures and glue them to pieces of construction paper. Next tell the children to make the following labels and attach them to a large piece of poster board: LAND, LABOR, CAPITAL, and ENTREPRENEURSHIP. After all the pictures have been placed around the poster board, tell students to use a piece of string to connect each one to the appropriate label.

Definition of Factors of Production

✢ **Land**—natural resources such as water, soil, trees, and minerals

✢ **Labor**—workers, talents, training, skills

✢ **Capital**—buildings, factories, machinery, tools, vehicles, equipment

✢ **Entrepreneurship**—owners, organizers, profit seekers, top decision makers, investors

(Teacher Tip) You might want to display student work on a bulletin board or in the hallway.

49 Branches of Government Chain

This activity will help students organize and understand the three branches of government and their functions.

MATERIALS

Colored paper, scissors, stapler or glue sticks, markers, and yarn or string

WHAT TO DO

First, have students cut the colored paper into long strips to make a paper chain. Instruct them to use different colors for each of the three branches. After connecting the sections, tell students to write down the duties of the President, Congress, and the Supreme Court on separate pieces of paper. Then have them attach each job to the branch of government that performs it. The color coding should help students to recall the role of each branch in the operation of our government.

(Teacher Tip) This activity can also be used to help students understand such forms of government as monarchy, dictatorship, and democracy.

50 Hanger Mobile— Branches of Government

This activity is yet another way to help students better understand the organization of our system of government.

MATERIALS

Clothes hangers, paper, scissors, glue sticks or stapler, pencils, crayons or markers, and pieces of yarn or string

WHAT TO DO

Students should label paper with the three branches of government and glue or staple them to the bottom of a clothes hanger. On separate pieces of paper, have the children list the powers of each branch and attach them with yarn or string to the correct heading. As in the previous activity, color-coding each branch will help students gain a better understanding of the American system of government.

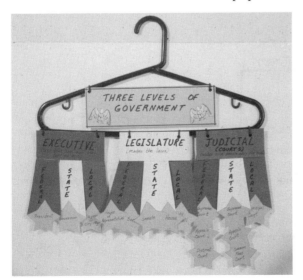

(Teacher Tip) This project can also be used with such different forms of government as monarchy, dictatorship, and democracy. You might want to display the completed hangers in the classroom or in the hallway.

Four-Flap Book

1. Fold paper in thirds the long way.

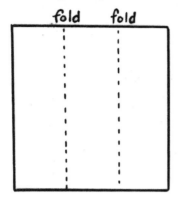

2. Open paper and fold in thirds in the opposite direction.

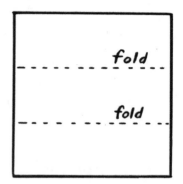

3. Open paper and cut off the four corner boxes.

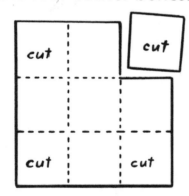

4. Refold the four flaps.

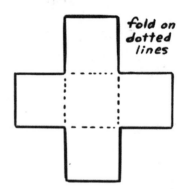

5. Number each flap as the flap book is opened.

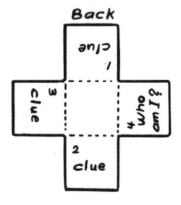

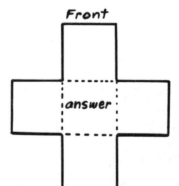

all flaps folded in

Super Social Studies Scholastic Professional Books, 1999

Name______________________________ Date__________________

State Bookmark

After you fill in the blanks, cut out the bookmark. Follow your teachers instructions for adding a map at the top.

State ____________

Origin of Name ____________

Capital ____________

Admitted to the Union ______

Motto ____________

Song ____________

Flower ____________

Bird ____________

Tree ____________

Major Cities ____________

____

Major Rivers ____________

____

Goods and Services ____________

____

____

Super Social Studies Scholastic Professional Books, 1999

Step Book

Here's how to make a step book:

1. Determine the number of pages you want in your step book. (For each fold, you will have 2 step book pages.)

2. Fold the first sheet, leaving a $1/2$" – $3/4$" border.

3. Now place this sheet on top of a second folded sheet on which you also have a $1/2$" – $3/4$" border.

4. Repeat until the desired number of sheets is used.

5. Fasten the top with two staples.

6. Organize your step book by labeling each of the borders.

1 fold

2 folds

3 folds

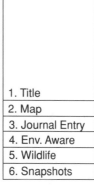

| 1. Title |
| 2. Map |
| 3. Journal Entry |
| 4. Env. Aware |
| 5. Wildlife |
| 6. Snapshots |

Making a Triorama

Follow the directions below to make a triorama.

1. Fold the top left corner of a piece of 8 1/2-by-14-inch construction paper diagonally so that the top edge of the paper is flush with the right edge of the paper.

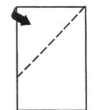

2. Fold the top right corner diagonally so that it touches the lower point of the previous fold.

3. Fold the panel at the bottom to make a horizontal crease along the edge. Cut off this section.

4. Open the paper up and cut along the lower-left diagonal crease to the center of the paper.

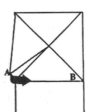

5. Pull point A over to point B so that the piece you cut is flush with the lower right diagonal crease. Glue the base into place.

* Making a Super Triorama

Four trioramas can be glued together to form a pyramid.

* Designing the Inside

Design the inside scenes of the triorama using any available craft materials—construction paper, string, fabric scraps, cotton balls, markers, and crayons—to make the scene three-dimensional. Write a brief paragraph describing the scene along the bottom flap. Make guidelines by lightly drawing pencil lines on the flap and then erasing the lines after writing the paragraph.

Super Social Studies Scholastic Professional Books, 1999

Significant Individual

Write a summary on the back of this paper. Include the information from below.

What cultural group (national origin, race, gender, age, ethnicity, religion) does the individual belong to?

What is the individual like?

Individual's name

_____

Draw a picture of the person.

List contributions of achievements of the individual.

Tell some interesting facts about the individual.

Super Social Studies Scholastic Professional Books, 1999

Snapshot Frames

Use this page to make a snapshot book.

Super Social Studies Scholastic Professional Books, 1999

Artifacts

Tell about your artifact by answering these questions.

What is it made of?

How old is it?

What is it?

What was it used for? OR
How was it used?

Was it made by hand or mass
produced?

Would you have ever used it?

Is it used today?

Super Social Studies Scholastic Professional Books, 1999

Notes

Notes